DROWNING IN MY THOUGHTS

POEMS BY
THERESA HOOKS

Table of Content

Acknowledgment

I would like to acknowledge **Jesus Christ**, my Lord and Savior. With Him, all things are possible.

I dedicate this book to the quiet moments that sparked inspiration and
to the untold stories that continue to fuel our aspirations.

1 Peter 5:6

"Humble yourselves, therefore, under God's mighty hand, that He may lift you up in due time."

In Your Hands

God, you changed my life

I'm no longer blue

My Life is filled with happiness

And I owe it all to you

You took away the pain and all the things

That made my house incomplete

Then filled it with joy and love

And your mercy that's oh so sweet

Lord, I have to say thank you

And I hope you understand

You are my whole world

And my life is in your hands

The Only One I Can Trust

I sit alone with tears in my eyes

Thinking I just don't understand

You are here one minute, the next you are gone

I wish I knew your plans

It's like I don't know you

Not anymore

Are you my lover, my husband

The one that I adore

You've changed so much

In a short amount of time

Your plans for my heart

Is what's been on my mind

You said you would never hurt me

I put my trust in you

But it's happening again

And this makes number two

By this, I see that your love

Will one day turn to dust

And that God is the only one

That I can really trust

A Love Beyond Compare

I changed my life for the better

I hope you're proud of me

To what me and my God have

Nothing can compete

Although I have a new Love

I still care for you

I'll be yours forever

God gave me to you

Fake Friends

Roses are red

The sky is blue.

I know who I am.

But who are you

Are you my friend

Or are you my foe

You tell me

'Cause I don't know

A true friend is true

Not Fony or Fake

Are you a true friend

What do you say

You say you are

But that's just words

The actions you showed

Was all I heard

Make no mistake

Your words don't phase me

Because the stuff you say

Sounds real crazy

A friend like you

I don't need

What you need to do

Is get on your knees

And pray to God

That he may forgive

Then focus on your own life

The one that you live

Do You Love Me

Do you love me

I don't know

Your actions, I see

Really don't show

I dedicated my life

To loving you

But breaking my heart

Is all you seem to do

If you love someone

Shouldn't you show it

Love her hard

And make her know it

What happened to your love

Did you lose it somewhere

Or is it that

You love someone else

Is it your friends

That makes you choose '

Cause hanging with them

Is all you do

Do you love me

I can't tell

It feels like your love

Has gone to hell

I feel so discouraged

What am I to do

My heart will break into pieces

If I lose my love from you

Tell me, do you love me

Please tell me the truth

Because from the answer you give me

I'll know what to do

Cherish What You Have

How would you feel

If you were all alone

You wake up one day

And your love mate is gone

You sit and think

About all the time you wasted

You should've told her how you felt

But you hesitated

You should've kissed and held her close

But now it's much too late

She's gone out of your life

Left without a trace

If you could do it over

This time, you'd show her

How much you really care

You'd spend some time

And always be right there

My suggestion to you is that you thank

The Lord for what you have today

Do all you can to make sure

That your love mate doesn't go away

When They Grow

My kids are my life
That's why I think twice
About everything I do

I give them advice
And dress them up nice
And that keeps me smiling too

I love my boys
They bring me joy
They're everything I am about

They'll forget their toys
They'll grow from boys
They'll be men without a doubt

I hate to see the day
When they grow up and say
Mom I'm moving away

I'll say a prayer
on this sad day
They'll be in God's hands
So I know they'll be ok

Lies

Your lies will catch up to you
Just you wait and see
You're just lying to yourself
Because you're not lying to me
You can say whatever you want
But God knows the truth
And when it's time for judgement
It'll all fall back on you
You hurt the people who love you
And it doesn't even matter
Every time you open your mouth
The lies keep getting fatter
Why don't you stop and think about it
What do you really gain
When it's all said and done
The facts remain the same
Your lies will bring you pain one day
This I know without guessing
So I looked up to heaven and prayed
That God will pour you down a blessing

I Passed the Test

Look at me
I made it through
I took the path
God told me to
He took my hand
And led me on
He gave me strength
To make me strong
He told me that life
Was full of surprises
And that the devil's tricks
I shouldn't take lightly
But to keep my prayers
And stay strong in my faith
And the enemy's presence
Will soon be erased
He told me that the pain
Would soon fade
Just stay on the road
That he has made
He said love your neighbor
Like I love you
And you will get your blessing
That's long over due
He helped me to make it
To the better side
I'll be praising him
Until the day I die

Riding with Faith

Riding in my drop top
Cooling my brain
Listening to my girl Cece
Again and again
Man I'm just chillin
You know what I mean
I'm not high, I'm not low
Just in between
Cruzin on my twenties
Spreewells chromed out
The plates in the back
Say munchie without a doubt
Gutted out white leather
You know what I mean
With a purple candy paint
That's oh so clean
I'm swerving in my Suburban
Just doing my job
Enjoying my life
And thankful to God
I don't get high
And I don't get drunk
Just rolling with Jesus
Keeping it Crunk

Drugs

Drugs is an epidemic
That rules the world
They don't discriminate
They take boy or girl
They come in different shapes
Colors, fashions, and forms
They'll get you high
But they cause you harm
They are sometimes called medicine
But they're not the same
Medicine heals the body
Drugs kill the brain
Marijuana works on the cells
Crack breaks the heart
Speed knocks you down
Before you can start
Powder makes your nose
Bloody red
Heroin stops the veins
Kills them dead
All kinds will kill you
That's no lie
Stay away from drugs
If you don't want to die

Letter to God

Dear Lord,

We finally made it; thanks to you
We took the path you told us to
The road got rough a long the way
But you carried us with your love and grace
You gave us strength; that made us strong
You showed us mercy the whole while long
For the experience we've shared, and the lives we've touched
Just saying thank you would not be enough
Life with you Lord is like a recovering drug abuser
You must let go of the past and deal with the future
So as we go our separate ways; we can let go of our fears
Because we know Lord; that you will always be near
When we get discouraged or become afraid
We'll just stay on the path that you have made
For those that don't know you; I pray they will see
So open up their hearts, that they might receive
Thank you for your promises; as we've all heard
You will give us the desires of our hearts; if we stay in your word
To each and everyone of you; I pray for peace in your life
And hope that one day; you will all come to know Christ

Amen

In the Presence of God

So much darkness all around
The noise is so loud
My heart it fastly pounds
Wake me from this nightmare
It feels so real
the touch on my shoulder
It gives my soul chills
I asked who are you
The voice I heard was surely real
I am the Lord, God Almighty
Rise up and see
Bow down my child and worship me
Now I'm on the floor
Looking up to heaven
Asking God to send me a blessing
For my heart is heavy
So much hurt and chaos in my life
My eyes are blinded by all of the strife
Awaken he said so you can see
Everything in this world belongs to me
You are my child
And I love you so much
If you submit all to me Your heart I will touch
Thank you. God
Is all I could say
while all of my worries
Faded away

Yesterday Is Gone

Looking out the window
Watching life pass by
Today is already gone
And tomorrow will fly
Where did time go
I can't find it anywhere
Is it hiding in the closet
Or is it under the chair
Thinking back on my life
All the pain and disrespect
God said hold on my child
I am not finished with you yet
Grab hold my hand and
Forget about yesterday
Tomorrow is full of Joy
And it is on the way

Faith

God will do it for you
Do you believe
You only need faith
The size of a mustard seed
Faith without works is surely dead
And the thing you're praying for
Will fall on it's head
Did you accept Jesus into your heart
I should have started off
With that part
Love him, accept him
Pray and read
Then the desires of your heart
You can receive

From Pain to Praise

My life hasn't been easy
It's been full of lies
It's been full of hurt and pain
It's been full of cries
It's been full of betrayal
It's been full of deceit
It's been full of disappointments
It's been full of defeat
It's been full of let downs
It's been full of turned backs
It's been full of heartache
It's been full of Lack
It's been full of Loss money
It's been full of loss Jobs
It's been full of praying and calling out to God
It's been a lot of fasting
It's been a lot of on my knees
It's been a lot of raising my hands
It's been a lot of release
Now It's a lot of Joy
Now it's a lot of Peace
Now its a lot of giving it to God
And yes I do believe
The way I move
The way I talk
The things I say
The walk I walk
The way I love
The way I give
The way I pray
The way I live
The way I read
The way I share
Go against God's word
I wouldn't dare
God Is my life
God is the reason
Not just today
But every season
Thank you God for saving me

Thank you God for delivering me
Thank you God for showing me
All of the things I couldn't see
Thank you for removing people
That meant me no good
Thank you for opening my mind
To things I misunderstood
Thank you for your mercy
Thank you for your grace
In my heart, Dear Lord
You will always have a place

Not Today Devil

Today is not the day devil
I don't have time for your stress
I rebuke you in the name of Jesus
Now go on with your mess

I submit myself to God
So you have to flee
Get all your snares and all your traps
And go far away from me

My mind is sober
I am very alert
The little tricks you try
They will not work

I'm covered in the blood
And I stand firm in my faith
You can keep trying if you like
But it's your time you waste

Away from me Satan
Away you go
Don't come back around here
Snooping no more

My armor is on
My guard is up
I'm not listening to your lies
So you can shut up

Away from me Satan
Get away from me

God is my Vindicator
And he is protecting me

Rebuke The Devil

The devil is a liar
Can't you see
He will tell you all the things
That you can't be

He will whisper in your ear
Kill, steal, destroy
And when he's done with you
He'll treat you like an old toy

I can tell you how to beat him
If you want to know
Pay very close attention
I will go slow

The Bible should be your reference
The words should be your sword
For all the information in there
Is from the mouth of God

Standing firm in God's word
Is what you have to do
Integrity and honesty
That's called the Belt of Truth

Protect your mind from negative thoughts
With God have open communication
This kind of protection symbolizes hope
It's called the Helmet of Salvation

Put your trust in God
And don't be haste
Extinguish fiery darts
This is called the Shield of Faith

Are you ready to spread God's word
Get up on your feet
Slip on your shoes
The Gospel of Peace

Protect your heart from evil
Get rid of all viciousness
Then you will be able to put on
The Breastplate of Righteousness

Now that I've told you
Everything you need to do
Put on your armor everyday
And trample the devil under your shoe

MOMA

You were not perfect
That I understand
You did the best you could
With what was in your hand

I appreciate you
And everything you did
The way you took care of me
When I was a little kid

I love you so much
I just want you to know
From the top of your head
To the bottom of your toe

You have taught me a lot
For that I say thank you
And to myself
I will always be true

I pray God bless you
And that's no lie
I will be here for you
Until the day I die

Through The Fire

God gave me a lover
Who would never love me back
I was confused at first
Thinking why would God do that

I loved unconditionally
Like God told me to
He always seemed to hurt me
No matter what I'd do

He would lay with other women
And not just a few
Not even realizing
The punishment he'd be due

He would hang out with his friends
Leaving me at home
Gone all the time
Leaving me alone

With tears in my eyes
He would lie to my face
All the things he did
Was just a disgrace

Who forgets their anniversary
Not even a card
But for every important date
I would always go hard

Treat me better
I cried and pleaded
Because if you don't
One day I'm leaving

I went back to God
I can't take no more
Do something please
My heart is on the floor

God told me to be patient
For He had a plan
To keep my faith
My life is in His hands

47

I kept on loving him
Broken and confused
I kept on doing
What God told me to

He treated others perfect
But treated me like trash
He even got tricked with some witchcraft

It wasn't just him
There were others too
My friends, my family
A bunch of different groups

Then God stepped in
Said enough is enough
Told me to separate
Cause it's about to get rough

I fasted and I prayed
I stayed in my Word
God revealed to me
Everything He heard

He said, vengeance is mine
For each one of them
Told me not to lift a finger
They are already condemned

God gave them time to repent
But they still refused
Now everything they cherish
They are about to lose

They all laughed
They all made fun
God told them don't touch
His anointed one

Now I understand
Why God made me stay
All of my hurt
Was not in vain

The cults and secret societies
He wanted to expose
Everything they had going on
Only God knows

That's no longer my concern
I'm happy over here
God is the head of my life
He's the only one I fear

Waiting for my True Love
Reading, studying and praying
God will send him in time
And I know he won't delay him

Thank you God for everything
I love you with all my heart
Loving on myself from now on
And today I'm going to start

Daddy

I was 6 years old
When God took him home
My daddy passed away
And left me alone

I couldn't understand
How could this be
I'm his only child
How could he leave me

I knew before they told me
No one would listen
At that early age
I was using my intuition

My heart was so broken
I lost my self-esteem
I wish I could wake up
And it all be a dream

He was my life
And I loved him so much
How could I keep living
I almost gave up

Growing up without him
Was so very hard
All I knew to do
Was call on the Lord

It took a long time
To release this pain
God mended my heart
And renewed my brain

He held me tight
And comforted me
I held Him back
Knowing He would never leave

Guidance

When you need guidance
And you don't know what to do
Just call on the Lord
And He will see you through

God, direct my path
And show me Your way
Walk beside me, dear Lord
So I don't go astray

Guide me in Your truth
And clear my vision
Bless me with Your grace
To make the right decision

Clear my mind
And remove barriers too
Remove everything, God
That prevents me from hearing You

Teach me how to act
For I put my trust in You
I lean not on my understanding
But in everything You do

When things don't go my way
Please help me to understand
For my best interest
Is always in Your plans

Peace

As I focus on my thoughts
Let peace fall on me
Still my burdened heart
Release my anxieties

You're not a God of disorder
I cast my cares on You
You promised me peace
I put my trust in You

This world causes stress
But I am of good cheer
For You have conquered the world
And no man will I fear

Wholeness and tranquility
Harmony and freedom too
Your covenant of peace
Shall not be removed

Forgiveness

Forgiveness is something
We all must endure
To receive God's forgiveness
We must do this for sure

It's not about forgetting
But letting things go
Giving it to God
So your love can grow

He will take away the hurt
He will take away the pain
He will fill you with His Spirit
So you can trust again

If you're harboring unforgiveness
I pray you release it
Ask God for strength
He cannot be defeated

Ask Him for grace
He will refine your heart
But ask Him for your own forgiveness
We all have to do our part

Family Business

I love my family
But some don't love me
Turn their backs and betray
Lord, how could this be

Who can I depend on?
Surely none of them
God is the head of my life
I can surely depend on Him

I just don't understand
I would give my last
They would take me for granted
And behind my back they laugh

While I poured out my heart
With all the love I possess
Instead of loving me back
They crushed me with stress

I love my family
No matter what they do
But loving on myself
Is what I've learned too

I forgive everyone
And I hope they forgive me
But putting myself first
Is how it's going to be

I will love some from afar
And love some close-up
The love in my heart
I will not allow them to touch

I ask God to bless them
Show them His ways
Fill them with His love
And lengthen their days

I know that I am loved
The love of Jesus Christ
He loves me unconditionally
For He laid down His life

I will forever love my family
Yes, I will indeed
But at the end of the day
Jesus is all I need

Panic Attack

Why am I going through this again
As I stand here clutching my chest
I can feel my throat closing up
I can hear my heavy breath

Sweat runs down my face
As tears form in my eyes
Anxiety takes hold of me
As my fear intensifies

I whispered for help
My voice shaky and weak
As I laid on the floor
No one could hear me speak

I cried out to God
Lord, help me please
Can you send someone
Here to rescue me

I closed my eyes
This must be the end
God, please forgive me
For all of my sins

Somebody lifted me up
And to my surprise
God sent me an angel
To save my life

Thank You, dear Lord
You did it again

I pray in Jesus' name
These panic attacks will end

Jealousy

Why do you hate me so much
What did I ever do to you
I showed up when you needed me
I always came through

Why are you so envious
I don't have a lot
And you can keep what you have
I don't want what you got

Are you feeling unworthy
Why are you so insecure
The way that you gossip
Is really immature

Always trying to make me look bad
You're really overzealous
Try so hard to outdo me
I really think you're jealous

Jealousy is a sin
It's really a toxic trait
If you don't get some help
It could turn into hate

I pray God open your eyes
So that you can really see
What He made in you
Is really something unique

And that you love yourself
For who you are
You are very special
Baby, you are a star

Abigail

The Father's joy, beautiful and wise
Nabal was evil and uncouth
She loved God and she was faithful
But she was married to a fool

David was anointed by God
And destined for the throne
Out in the desert protecting the sheep
He left Nabal's shepherds alone

David's men went to Nabal
Asking for food and drink
Nabal, who was rich in the land
Turned them away without a blink

David was mad, furious even
He gathered his men and grabbed his sword
And headed to Nabal's kingdom

Abigail stepped in and made things right
Nabal soon passed away
And David made her his wife

1 Samuel 25

Rahab

Strolling through the Jericho streets
Everyone looks upon her
But nobody ever speaks

They call her harlot
But not by her name
At night, a knock on her door
Appeared two spies with no shame

God commanded
Jericho must fall
"Since I hide you
Please save me, my family, and all

Hang a red ribbon on your door
And please follow the plan
Gather everyone in your home
And you all will surely stand"

Two messengers came looking
"Are the spies still here?"
She told them they fled
"By the gates they should be near"

Joshua and his army came around
For six days they marched
Around Jericho's grounds
And on the 7th day
God knocked the whole thing down

Only one house was still standing
When all was said and done
Rahab and her family was saved
And God was the victorious one

Scripture References:

- **Joshua 2:1–24**

- **Joshua 6:22–25**

- **Hebrews 11:31**

- **James 2:25**

- **Matthew 1:5**

- **Psalm 89:10**

- **Isaiah 51:9**

Esther

Hadassah, born a Jew and raised
By her cousin Mordecai
She had great faith with beauty and grace
She caught Hegai's eye

She married Xerxes the king
Then she became Queen
But kept her identity hidden
As Jews in the Persian kingdom
She feared was forbidden

Haman plotted to kill the king
And kill all the Jews
She approached the king strategically
To give him the disturbing news

When Haman found out her identity
He bowed down at her feet
The king got very angry
And ordered him deceased

Mordecai saved the king's life
By exposing Haman's plot
After Haman was put to death
Mordecai got Haman's spot

Hadassah saved her people
Yes, she was a contestant
But now she's no longer Hadassah
They call her Queen Esther

Esther

- **Esther 4:16**

- **Esther 7:3**

- **Esther 8:6**

Miriam

All boys to be thrown in the river
As ordered by Pharaoh
Moses floated in a basket while his sister watched
As she couldn't let him go

Pharaoh's daughter found him
And made him her own
She gave him back to Miriam
To be raised in her home

She led the women with sing and dance
After Pharaoh died in the sea
They sang to the Lord and exalted His name
While beating their tambourines

She was jealous of Moses' wife
And questioned his mastery
That made God very angry
He struck her with leprosy

Praying and interceding
On his knees Moses kneeled
After 7 days outside the camp
God let Miriam heal

Scripture References:

- **Exodus 2:4–10**

- **Exodus 15:20–21**

- **Numbers 12:1–15**

- **Numbers 26:59**

- **Micah 6:4**

Ruth

A Moabite woman who committed
To her mother-in-law after her husband died
"Your God is my God, wherever you go I will follow
Until the day I die"

Back in Bethlehem she picked up
Leftover grain in the field
Boaz, who owned it, saw her there
And gave her a sweet deal

She worked and ate with the other workers
So she wouldn't be alone
He gave her plenteous grain
That she took to Naomi back home

She laid at his feet and asked him
To marry her hand
He was pleased and also shocked
That she chose him out of all the men in the land

He said, "It would be my pleasure
But I am not next in kin
I will ask the kinsman-redeemer
If he refuse, I will marry you then"

Since the kinsman-redeemer refused
He took Ruth for his wife
They had a son called Obed

And they lived a happy life.

Ruth

Ruth 1:16–17

Deborah

A prophetess and judge
Known for her wisdom and discernment
People from all over Israel
Came to her for guidance and judgment

Guided by God, she was a
Wise and courageous leader
She instructed Barak to gather 10,000 men
To go up against Sisera

Barak was scared but said he'd go
Only if she went with him
She agreed to go but prophesied
That Sisera would be killed by a woman

The day of the battle arrived
And Deborah stood beside him
God stepped in with water
And defeated all of them

But Sisera somehow escaped
Not knowing he would soon meet his fate

Scripture References:

- **Judges 4 and 5**

- **Judges 5**

Jael

Kenite woman who took sides
With the Israelites
Sisera escaped and ran to her tent
And she welcomed him with delight

She gave him milk and allowed
Him to rest in her bed
When he was fast asleep
She drove a peg through his head

Barak came looking for him
And she led him into her home
There lay Sisera in her bed
Not asleep but dead and gone

A woman killed him just as
Deborah prophesied
That led into a victory
For all of the Israelites

Scripture References:

- **Judges 4:17–22**

- **Judges 5:24–27**

Mary Magdalene

While spreading God's word
Jesus did travel about
She possessed 7 demons
And He did cast them out

She picked up her cross
And followed His principle
She was no longer a sinner
And she became His disciple

While following Him
She cared for His needs
When He was crucified
She fell to her knees

She went to anoint Jesus' body
In the tomb where He lay
His body was not there
As it was the third day

An angel told her
"Go tell the disciples what you see
For He has gone ahead of you
Into Galilee"

He first appeared to her
On the first day of the week
She went and told the others
But nobody would believe

While they were gathered
He appeared to the eleven
Jesus told them to go tell the world
Then God took Him into heaven

Scripture References:

- **Matthew 27:56, 61**

- **Matthew 28:1**

- **Mark 15:40, 47**

- **Mark 16:1–11**

- **Luke 8:2**

- **Luke 24:10**
- **John 19:25**
- **John 20:1–18**

Eve

First woman created, Created
from Adam's rib
In the Garden of Eden
Paradise is where she lived

With her husband Adam
They had all they need
God told them not to eat
Anything from the forbidden tree

In the middle of the garden
Is where it stood
Along came the serpent
He was up to no good

"Eat, Eve, eat, you will not die
You will be like God
For He is very wise"

She took fruit from the tree
She ate it and it was delicious
She gave some to Adam
He wasn't even suspicious

They looked at each other
Nakedness is all they see
When God called for them
They hid, and He was not pleased

Because of their disobedience
He cursed them both
Out of the Garden of Eden
All of them must go

Serpent will crawl on his belly
All the days of his life
Between him and human
Will always be strife

Eve to have pain
While giving birth
Her husband to be the head
While on this earth
Adam is to struggle

By the sweat of his brows
This is to go on until
They return to the ground

Scripture References:

- **Genesis 2 & 3**

- **2 Corinthians 11:3**

- **1 Timothy 2:13**

Hagar

Egyptian maidservant
To her mistress Sarai
Who gave her to her husband Abram
To have them a child

For Sarai was infertile
And she wanted a family bad
She felt like her servant Hagar
Was the only choice she had

Abram laid with her
And a child she did conceive
When she realized she was pregnant
Being superior to Sarai is what she perceived

Sarai went to Abram
Feeling hurt and upset
"She is your maidservant
Do what you think is best"

She ran away from Sarai
Because she treated her bad
By the springs an angel found her
And told her to go back

She had a son and named him Ishmael
As Beer-Lahai-Roi told her
She gave God this name
For in the desert He saw her

Sarai had a son Isaac
Like God said she would
She sent Hagar and Ishmael away
Back out into the woods

Out in the desert
Their water ran dry
She watched her son thirst
And they started to cry

God called down from heaven
"Hagar, no need to be afraid
Look at the water well
That I have made

Lift the boy up
Take him by the hand
I will make him a great nation
In all of the land"

Scripture References:

- **Genesis 16**

- **Genesis 21**

- **Galatians 4:21–31**

Mary

To give birth to Jesus
She was chosen by God
With her being a virgin
She thought this was hard

She was engaged to Joseph
But he couldn't understand
How could she be with child
Without laying with a man

An angel appeared to him
Told him to marry this girl
As the child she is carrying
Will save the world

They traveled to Bethlehem
Joseph's ancestral town
Jesus was born in a stable
And shepherds came from all around

They saw His star in the east
And came bearing gifts
They saw Him there with Mary
And bowed down to worship Him

She saw her Son get crucified
Right before her eyes
She kneeled down at the cross
And watched her Son die

On the 3rd day He rose
He lives in the Church

And the Church lives
In each one of us

Scripture References:

- **Luke 1:26–56**

- **Luke 2:19**

- **Luke 2:51**

- **John 2:1–12**

- **Matthew 1:18–25**

- **Luke 2:34–35**

- **John 19:25–27**

- **Acts 1:14**

Jochebed

Levite woman living in Egypt
She gave birth to a son
Pharaoh ordered to kill newborn males
For fear the population would overrun

She hid him for 3 months
But he started getting bigger
She put him in a basket
And sent him down the Nile River

Pharaoh's daughter found him
She wanted him for her own
She sent him back to Jochebed
To nurse him in her home

At a young age she gave him up
She couldn't raise him to a man
For giving him to Pharaoh's daughter
Was all a part of the plan

He'd live a life of royalty
Surrounded by many roses
Because she found him in water
Pharaoh's daughter called him Moses

Scripture References:

- **Exodus 2:1–10**

- **Exodus 6:20**

- **Numbers 26:59**

Rebekah

She came to the well when the servant arrived
She offered him water and his camels too
Just what he had prayed for
God has came through
He brought her back to Isaac
It was love at first sight
Since God gave his blessing
Isaac made her his wife

After they were married
His mom soon died
Isaac loved Rebekah so much
She brought comfort in his eyes

She had twin boys
Esau and Jacob
The Lord told her
They'd become 2 nations

Isaac favored Esau
Because he was a skillful hunter
Rebekah favored Jacob
As he was always with his mother

Esau was very hungry
He asked Jacob for some stew
Jacob said sell me your birthright
And I will give it to you

Rebekah made Jacob
Pretend to be Esau

As Isaac was blind
He'd bless him in the Lord
Before he lay down to die

When Isaac found out
He was really stressing
As Jacob came deceitfully
And stole Esau's blessing

Esau vowed to kill Jacob
Rebekah made him run
She vowed to send for him later

But that day would never come

Jacob and Esau reunited
With no conflicts in the way
Rebekah didn't witness this
As she had passed away

Genesis 24–27

Genesis 49:31

Anna the Prophetess

She dedicated her life to God
She worshipped day and night
As she never left the temple
She was there when baby Jesus arrived

She recognized him
As the long-awaited Messiah
She would tell everyone that listens
That was her desire

Luke 2:36–38

Elizabeth

Well in her years she wanted a son
But she was barren and couldn't have none

Her husband Zechariah
Prayed to God under the sun

Then an angel appeared with the
News of a child named John

Zechariah didn't believe
The angel took away his speech

When the child was born
His speech was released

He prophesied about his son
Preparing the way for the Messiah

He would later baptize Jesus
And that was God's desire

Luke 1

Rachel

She was the 2nd wife of Jacob
Her sister Leah was number one
She was very jealous of her
As she gave Jacob 6 sons

Jacob loved Rachel more
But that didn't matter
Not able to have his son
She couldn't even fathom

God remembered her
And opened up her womb
Now she'd get pregnant
And bare a son soon

His name will be called Joseph
Signifying her belief
God removed her shame
And that was great relief

She became pregnant again
It was hard labor at best
The birth of her son Benjamin
Took her to her death

Genesis 29:17–18

Genesis 29:30

Genesis 30:1

Genesis 30:6

Genesis 30:22–24

Genesis 35:16–20

Leah

The unseen wife of Jacob
Who was his first wife
He was tricked into marrying her
But Rachel was his life

Her eyes were weak
And Jacob wanted none
She was still faithful to him
And gave him 6 sons

She gave him a daughter named Dinah
Not too long after
He ended up marrying Rachel
To him that's all that matter

Genesis 29

Hannah

Was one of 2 wives to Elkanah
The other wife was named Peninnah
Peninnah had kids but Hannah had none
And for that every day Peninnah made fun

Hannah prayed to God
To give her a son
She'd give him back to the Lord
If He gave her one

God blessed her with a child
After hearing her plea
And when Samuel was old enough
She brought him to the priest

Since she kept her word
God blessed her, yes He did
She ended up having 5 more kids

She was so happy
She gave God praise
She would sing her song of prayer
For the rest of her days

1. Samuel 1 and 2

Bathsheba

Wife of Uriah the Hittite
King David saw her afar
She was very beautiful
And he wanted her

He knew she was married
But that was just a blur
He summoned her to his bed And there he laid with her

Uriah was fighting a war
While they had an affair
Bathsheba became pregnant
Oh what despair

David called Uriah home
To stay for a while
And sleep with his wife
To make him think it's his child

But when he refused
David had him killed
After Bathsheba mourned
As husband and wife they did live

The first child she had
Died because of David's sins
But soon after that
She had 4 more kids

1. Samuel 11 and 12

   1 Kings 1

Martha

Sister to Mary and Lazarus
Known for her strong faith
She was a disciple of Jesus
She welcomed him without haste

She was busy cooking and serving
While Mary sat at his feet
"I'm doing all the work
Jesus, why can't you see?"

"She chose the better part," he said
"By sitting, listening to me."

Lazarus got deathly sick
They sent for Jesus to pray
4 days later he came
But he had already passed away

Jesus saw Lazarus laying there
And yes he did weep
Then he prayed to God
And told Lazarus to get up on his feet

Martha had great faith
No one could ever doubt it
For when Jesus resurrected him
She lifted her hands and shouted

Luke 10:38–42

John 11:1–44

John 12:1–8

Priscilla

Married to Aquila and they both made tents
Being forced to leave Rome
They fled to Corinth

There they were faithful to follow Jesus Christ
They taught whoever would listen
Even if it would cost them their life

They met a mentor named Paul
And they were tent makers like him
They all worked together and he stayed with them

Tent makers by day
Teaching God's word by night
Helping anyone who'd listen to come to know Christ

She met a preacher named Apollo
Who didn't understand the doctrine
For he only spoke of John the Baptist
And not of Jesus' resurrection

They welcomed him into their home
And took him aside privately
They explained the way of God
To him more accurately

After they left Ephesus
They moved back to Rome
There they continued their ministry
And opened up a church
In their home

Acts 18:2–3

Acts 18:18

Acts 18:24–26

Romans 16:3–4

1. Corinthians 16:19

2. Timothy 4:19

Lydia

A wealthy businesswoman
Seller of purple cloth
She also told the future
To other people with cost

She followed Paul proclaiming
"He's telling you how to be saved"
She continued to worship God
And followed Paul for days

She listened to Paul preach
One day by the river
From the spirit of prediction
From her he did deliver

She was moved by his message
God opened her heart to believe
She and her family got baptized
And converted to Christianity

Acts 16:14–15

Acts 16:40

Huldah

A respected prophetess from Jerusalem
She understood God's will
In a world of national crisis
In God's presence she stood still

The Book of Law was found
But he couldn't understand it
King Josiah sought Huldah's wisdom
For her to explain it

"I will bring evil upon the place
Because they have forsaken me
But as for King Josiah
He did speak peace

Because of his obedience
God favored him
He would not feel the wrath
For as long as he lives"

2 Kings 22:14–20

2 Chronicles 34:22–28

Author Bio

Theresa Hooks (aka Munchie) from Enterprise, Alabama

Retired nurse, Military Veteran and Model

I started writing poetry in 1992. as a way of expressing my love for God and releasing emotions

I explore my faith in God in my poems

This book was inspired by my life experiences

I hope readers will take away from my poetry compassion for others and a commitment to effecting positive change

I think i have all 4 writing styles depending on what I'm writing

Theresa Hooks.

www.ingramcontent.com/pod-product-compliance
Lightning Source LLC
Chambersburg PA
CBHW051627140626
46547CB00033B/2754